Yell & Tell

By Debi Pearl

Sara Sue Learns To Yell & Tell

Copyright © December 2010 by Debi Pearl
ISBN: 978-1-61644-017-6

Published by No Greater Joy Ministries, Inc.
1000 Pearl Road, Pleasantville, TN 37033 USA

Written by Debi Pearl

Characters created by Debi Pearl

Illustrations by Benjamin Aprile

Painting by Michael Pearl

Layout by Lynne Hopwood

All scripture quotations are taken from the King James Holy Bible.

Sara Sue Learns To Yell & Tell may be purchased at a special discount for schools, universities, gifts, promotions, fund raising, or educational purposes. Licensing and rights agreements are available.

Printed in the United States of America by BookMasters, Inc.
30 Amberwood Parkway, Ashland, OH 44805
Jan 2011   M8156

Requests for information should be addressed to:
Mel Cohen, General Manager
No Greater Joy Ministries, Inc.
1000 Pearl Road
Pleasantville, TN 37033 USA
mcohen@nogreaterjoy.org
www.nogreaterjoy.org

NGJ ministries   A No Greater Joy Ministries Book

To little girls everywhere. Be safe!

– *Debi*

www.yellandtellbooks.com

2

Mama says, "Go out to play!"

    This is our very special day.

We'll swing and slide

    And sing along.

        Then beat our drums,

        DING and DONG.

We can both make puppets.

    It's easy as can be.

    I'll make one that looks like you,

    And you'll make one that looks like me.

I'm Sara Sue, I'll give you a CLUE.
Puppets are made with lots of glue.

Funny eyes, cute little noses,
A mouth for each that opens and closes.
Then fuzzy hair and brows that wiggle,
It's enough to make us giggle.

I'm Sara Sue, I have a CLUE.
I know things that can protect you.

This is something Mama told me
When I was just a little kid.
You should LISTEN very closely.
One day you'll be glad you did.

I'm Sara Sue, this is a CLUE.

Learn it because it's oh-so-true!

What's yours is yours,

What's mine is mine.

Remember that and you'll be fine.

Parts of your body are very special,

They are made for you alone.

No one else should ever touch them.

This rule should be set in stone.

Hey there, Little Pearlie!
Are you listening to my CLUES?
You should pay attention,
and learn what you can do!

Mama made our pantaloons,
And some for our puppets too.
They keep our bottoms covered;
It's the smartest thing to do.

We like our bloomers white
And our tights black as night,
But we'd rather wear our
PANTALOONS,
The green ones with the
RED BALLOONS.

11

I'm Sara Sue, and this is the CLUE.

You never know who's watching you.

When you climb up a ladder
Or slide down the slide
Or swing on a swing way up to the sky
Pantaloons will protect you
from peepers who are sly.

I'm Sara Sue, I have a CLUE.

You'll know someone's bad by what they do.

Sometimes bad things
Might catch you by surprise
Like when you're outside playing
And a friend comes strolling by.

He'll smile and say he likes you
And has a secret to tell,
Then take you someplace private
Where you'll be hidden really well.

You will know he is a bad boy
By the things he asks of you.
He'll want to touch your private parts
Which he's NOT allowed to do.

You should

RUN and TELL your mama,

She will know just what to do.

She will make that bad boy sorry

He ever tried to mess with you.

15

I'm Sara Sue, Here's another CLUE.

Telling Mama is a good thing to do.

It may be one of Mama's friends

Who says that you're a joy.

He seems like such a nice, nice man

When he gives you a shiny toy

He'll sit you tightly on his lap

Pretending that he cares.

But when no one else can see

He touches you down there.

It doesn't matter who the toucher is,

Big guy, little girl, brother or friend,

If anyone touches you like that

YELL and TELL

so he won't do it again.

I'm Sara Sue, I'm telling you

Don't wait a single minute,

Point your finger at the bad guy,

There's no way he can defend it.

YELL so loud and YELL so long

The cat will sing his lonesome song

Just like when we beat our drums

DING-a ling and ding-a DONG.

I'm Sara Sue, Here's the CLUE.

When you tell on a bad guy

And his secrets you reveal

Then other little children

Will be safer 'cause you squealed.

I'm Sara Sue, I've taught you clues.

Now you know just what to do.

Okay, my Little Pearlie,

I've done my very best,

But all you do is stare at me.

Have you learned anything yet?

I guess I need to show you

Just how it's to be done.

Scream your screechy,

creaky SCREAM

And tell your little feet to *RUN!*

22

26

I'm Sara Sue, remember this CLUE

So nothing bad happens to you.

What's yours is yours.

What's mine is mine.

No one else should touch or see.

Remember that and you'll be fine.

Now I ask you, Little Pearlie

Will you really scream that creaky scream?

That squeaky, screechy, squeally SCREAM?

The way you do when something really bothers you?

WOW!

That's a creaky, squeaky, squeally

SCREAM

That screechy scream will surely do!

You've really learned

to YELL and TELL.

I am so very proud of you.

I'm Sara Sue, with a clue for YOU.
You'll be safe now you know what to do!

I'll start right now and say it plain,
Listen, all you kids out there,
Protect yourself from ugly things.

Those prepared are usually spared!
It's really very simple.
All you need to know.
Learn to YELL and always TELL.

You've learned the

CLUES from Sara Sue.

Now it's time to review!

Clue 1. Knowing things will protect you.

Clue 2. What's yours is yours, no one should touch or see.

Clue 3. You never know who's watching you.

Clue 4. You'll know someone's bad by what they do.

Clue 5. You should run and tell your mama.

Clue 6. Others will be safer if you tell who is bad.

Clue 7. Those prepared are usually spared.

This is Sara Sue and little sister Pearlie;

We are counting on YOU!

Don't be embarrassed,

And never be afraid.

Always

YELL & TELL!

Mom and Dad, here's your CLUE: *Those prepared are usually spared.*

It is estimated that the average serial pedophile will molest 400 children during his lifetime. Molesters are usually just "regular Joes." Statistics tells us that 90% of all molestations are perpetrated by a relative or friend of the family. You teach your children to be wary of strangers, but what about your friends, brothers, or even Granddad?

Child molestation is sharply on the rise. Men who previously would never have considered such a perverse thing are now being inundated with pornography and conditioned to accept inordinate lusts. Further, in earlier years, where children were constantly under the watchful care of their mothers, today they are left in the hands of daycare workers and babysitters. Even the home is no longer a safe place with a constant stream of "Mama's friends." What hope do our little ones have?

To make matters worse, parents are uncomfortable talking to their children about the possibility of this ugly thing happening. In their effort to protect their children's innocence parents refrain from warning their children, leaving their kids totally unprepared against the sly, often familiar person who could be a child predator. In every area of life it is understood **that those prepared are usually spared**. Why leave our most precious treasures defenseless by not teaching them when and how to Yell and Tell?

Our children's best hope is having the knowledge provided by being forewarned. Knowledge gives the child power. It opens their eyes to the fact that even Mom and Dad might not know who the "bad guy" is. This awareness will keep a child from being gullible. When a potential predator says, "Don't tell," even a very small child will remember Sara Sue and her clues.

The *Yell & Tell* series was written to be a tool in a parent's hand, to make it convenient to reacquaint the child with the subject on a regular basis.

Stripping away his cover

A child predator loses his power when he loses his cover. *Yell & Tell* books are written to teach children and parents this critical fact. If all children knew that they would be heard and protected when they yelled and told, then many predators would never go child hunting.

Your children need to know that they can come to you any time and any place, and that you are ready to listen and take action to protect them. They will not understand this naturally; it is your responsibility as a parent to effectively communicate this message.

Child predators are professionals.

Predators know how to lie, how to make a child look silly, and how to make you feel embarrassed for even suggesting that they might be guilty of such a repulsive thing. Your child, on the other hand, is a child. He will feel ashamed, fearful, and uncertain, because his young conscience cannot bear such an evil thing.

A child predator might use his own children as decoys.

You need to understand that predators often use their own children to gain access to other children. The predator is most likely your friend or relative. Your children will like him. He will make you want to believe him, like him, and appreciate him. You briefly wonder if he is not entirely trustworthy, but the thought is so repulsive that you quickly put these evil thoughts behind you. And besides, it is so nice to have someone take the kids off your hands for an afternoon. It is a woeful exchange; you get a few hours of blessed peace, while your sweet three-year-old daughter loses her innocence and starts a life of brokenness inflicted on her by this "friend."

A child predator knows how to make your child feel responsible and guilty, effectively guaranteeing his or her silence. Most parents get so shaken at the thought of their child being molested that they make the mistake of asking questions with such intensity that the child panics and shuts down. Since the predator has already blemished the child's soul and mind, these poor kids are likely to be too fearful to tell the truth even in gentle questioning.

A parent MUST be proactive.

You must learn to look and listen. Watch your child. Watch FOR your child. Take a cue from Samuel's mama and ask "What if?" questions without making your child feel fearful that you are going to fuss at him or her. Remind your child of Sara Sue and her clues. Talk about the clues as you cook dinner or dress for school. These ideas need to stay fresh in your child's mind. Every few weeks read one of the *Yell & Tell* books aloud to your children.

A parent must be sacrificial.

Don't take the easy way out. Only leave your children with people you are positive are walking in truth. Just to be safe, go to several people who have known the person a long time and ask plainly, "Can you think of any reason why my child should not stay with this person?"

Let yourself be known as an unforgiving bear if anyone should ever touch your child. Other parents who don't understand the importance of these precautions may be offended at your questioning, but you must have friends who will help you protect your child, just like you would help protect theirs. In instances like this, it truly takes a tight community to avoid potentially harmful situations.

If there is a sexual predator in your circle of friends and family, and he hears you talking about warning your children, he will be reluctant to take a chance with your children. Predators look for the most vulnerable.

Don't be the devil's advocate.

Most parents like to avoid bringing this ugly thing to the attention of their social world. They simply don't want their child known as one who has been used, so they keep the matter under wraps—not only for their child's social protection, but for their own as well. The predator counts on parents keeping their mouths shut as much as he does the young victim. He will walk carefully for a few months, and then he will find another victim. Remember the statistic—400 victims per serial child predator.

Dress your child for safety.

As hideous as it seems, perverts love looking at the bottoms of tiny tots. Take caution to dress your little girl in fitting shorts under her dress, so as to thwart the sick peeping tom. Think about how normal men would respond to you in a short dress with your legs propped up showing your panties. Child predators are given a smorgasbord of lustful scenes on every playground and even in most church services. It is a chilling thought. As child pornography grows, so do the number of men who are lusting after small children. We must be proactive in dressing our vulnerable children.

Be wise, but not paranoid.

Most people are normal and are as horrified about the reality of child molestation as you are. The trouble is that perverts hide behind a normal looking face.

Most child molesters live out their lives in peace and success. No one ever tells on them, so no one ever knows except the silent broken trail of victims they leave behind. They feel safe because among all the children they have violated, not one has ever spoken out, even those who are now grown.

But someday there will surely be a day of judgment, when every perverse hunger will be revealed and they will face the terror of an angry God. I will be there watching, and I will rejoice when their calamity cometh.

Until that blessed day, read this book and the other *Yell & Tell* books to your children. Ask questions. Watch for signs of fear or anxiety in your child concerning any friends or family. Our children are given to us to protect and nurture. They need us. Tell your children every day, "I love you and want to keep you safe, so always tell me anything that needs to be told. I will always listen."